ONE MAN SHOW

Editorial cartoons by

DAVID HORSEY

Seattle Post-Intelligencer

Printed and bound in the United States of America.

ISBN 0-9624559-7-0

To order additional copies of *One Man Show* contact:

Public Affairs Department
Seattle Post-Intelligencer
101 Elliott Avenue West
Seattle, WA 98119

Telephone: (206) 448-8005

Other books by David Horsey:
Politics and Other Perversions (1974)
Horsey's Rude Awakenings (1981)
Horsey's Greatest Hits of the '80s (1989)
Cartooning AIDS Around the World (1992)
The Fall of Man (1994)

David Horsey's cartoons are distributed internationally by North America Syndicate.

Back cover photo: Larry Marcus
Design assistance: Duane Hoffmann

To Nole Ann

For the martini search in New York
and Vivaldi in Paris.

For the Inaugural Ball in '97
and the Lincoln Memorial on New Year's Eve.

For the warm days in Le Lavandou
and the happy days at Elm House.

For 10 a.m., February 2, 1983
and 10 p.m., May 16, 1984.

For Victoria, B.C.

For the senior prom.

For all the places, all the moments, all the love.

INTRODUCTION

By David Horsey
August 1999

I blame it on the Pulitzer.

One morning in June, I was flying in a small commuter airplane from Memphis to Chattanooga with tears welling up in my eyes. Not wanting to alarm the stranger wedged into the seat next to me, I looked away from the book I was reading and peered out the window down at the green Tennessee hills. I took a moment to calm my emotions, then began to read again. As soon as I did, the tears returned.

The book on my lap was *All Over but the Shoutin'* by New York Times reporter Rick Bragg. It's the story of his harrowing life growing up dirt poor in rural Alabama. It wasn't the tale of his hard times, though, that got me choked up. Rather, it was a later chapter in which he tells of taking his proud, long-suffering mother with him to Columbia University on the day he received his Pulitzer Prize.

Bragg described so well all that the occasion meant for him and his mother that, finally, I understood what the Prize meant for the people close to me. And I was terribly glad I had taken my own mom and my wife and kids along to New York City when the honor came my way.

I'm the kind of person who shuns histrionics. I don't wallow for long in depression. I don't stay angry for more than a flash. When things go well, I don't jump up and down, run in circles, scream and shout. Maybe that's because I'm used to things going well. I suppose it's also because, even at the highest moments, I have a strong sense of how fleeting are the glories of life.

It was March when I learned I was one of three finalists for the Pulitzer Prize in Editorial Cartooning. That meant I had a whole month to agonize before the winner was announced on April 12th. At first, I didn't even want to talk about it, fearing that some presumptuous comment I might make would float up into the atmosphere and set off a chain reaction of molecules that would imperceptibly shift the air breathed by the Pulitzer judges and turn their whims away from me.

The other two cartoonists nominated, Clay Bennett of the *Christian Science Monitor* and Rob Rogers of the *Pittsburgh Post-Gazette*, were friends whose work I admired. I figured my chances were no better than one-in-three and that meant I was likely to be passed over again, as I had been when I was a Pulitzer finalist in 1987. So I worked on enjoying my four weeks as a finalist while convincing myself I wouldn't be the lucky one this year.

Not that I didn't think I deserved it. I thought I did. But I also thought Rob and Clay would be just as deserving, as would several other practitioners of our peculiar brand of political commentary. There is seldom a single Best Editorial Cartoonist in any year, even though that's the accolade I won from the National Press Foundation for 1998. But, since somebody's got to win, I was perfectly willing to let it be me.

Still, I wasn't going to cancel my family's trip to Mexico that happened to coincide with the day of the announcement. So, on Friday, April 9th, I flew south. Then, on Sunday, April 11th, leaving behind wife and kids and friends and sand and sea and palm trees and margaritas, I flew back to Seattle to be in the *Post-Intelligencer* newsroom if lightning should strike.

And it did. At noon on the 12th the announcement came in. The phones started ringing, the champagne was uncorked, the celebration swirled around me. In the midst of the excitement, I remained relatively calm. I felt great satisfaction at rising to this pinnacle of my profession but knew full well how arbitrary and subjective any contest, including the Pulitzer, can be. I knew I was lucky to be chosen and wanted to bear the honor without a hint of hubris. I stayed cool.

Nevertheless, as the days went by, I began to marvel at the reaction to my Pulitzer in the world beyond the newsroom. Strangers on the street shouted congratulations. Old teachers, long-lost girlfriends, distant relatives, friends of my parents who remembered me as a freckle-faced kid who spent a lot of time with paper and pencil, people from every corner of my life and every part of town let me know how happy they were. This was not just a special moment for me, it was special for them.

And then, on that flight to Chattanooga, when I read what the Pulitzer had meant to one other lucky guy, I finally understood what it must mean to my own mother, how proud my father would have been if he had lived to see it, how it fit in with the story of my own family, the way winning this honor would be attached to my name and my people and my community for a long time to come. And the feeling was so humbling and so deep that tears were natural and unavoidable and, despite the embarrassment, welcome.

One Man Show

This book is another part of the celebration of what has been a very singular year in my life and career.

I've spent 20 years at the P-I concocting daily satires of the human drama. My previous collections covered 15 of those years. This one looks back on events since the Republican resurgence in the congressional elections of 1994. As with those other books, I sorted through hundreds of drawings to select this batch and was once again mortified by the high number of obvious rejects. It's lucky the Pulitzer committee didn't get a look at them. Even reading through the cartoons that made the final cut, some readers may find it difficult to understand why anyone has made such a fuss about me. Sometimes I am mystified, too. Yet, prize-worthy or not, this is what I was born to do. These pages are my current personal best.

The first short section of this book is a full-color "Brief History of the Millennium." I took on this project for the P-I editorial page as a way to mark civilization's passage into the 21st Century. Plus, it gave me an extra thousand years of human folly to lampoon.

The last color page features the elaborate cartoon that won me the National Press Foundation's Berryman Award. Altered slightly from the original to fit on a horizontal page, this image lends its title, "Beltway Apocalypse," to the entire second section of the book. These cartoons provide a visual chronicle of what has been one of the oddest chapters of American history. It's all there — the rise of Newt Gingrich, the Dole electoral doldrums, the obsession of Ken Starr, the humiliation of Hillary, the young intern in her thong, the unrelenting drive to impeachment which, in the event, was more damaging to Congress than to the mendacious, randy man in the Oval Office. I am not alone in suggesting I may well owe my Pulitzer to the eminently cartoonable weaknesses and amazing resilience of William Jefferson Clinton and so he is naturally the central character of this book.

The final half of this collection takes stock of America and the world at the end of the '90s. Titled "As the Century Turns," it encompasses everything beyond the Beltway, from Columbine to Kosovo, from Hollywood to Hong Kong, from the Third World to the cyber world, from Viagra sales to harpooning whales. It includes a pair of cartoons from my series on the Wenatchee witch hunt that also won notice from the Pulitzer panel and winds up with a second set of color pages portraying a "virtual" race for mayor of Seattle.

For anyone who really wants to know all my secrets, read on to the next page for "A Portrait of the Artist as a Pulitzer Prize Winner." Freelance-writer Erik Lundegaard caught me with my defenses down and produced this entertaining piece for *Washington Law & Politics* magazine. At the urging of my publisher, it is reprinted here.

I titled this latest collection *One Man Show* partly because this book constitutes a portable gallery of my art. The title is also descriptive of editorial cartooning. A single person does the research, frames the argument, writes the words, does the drawing and gets the credit or blame for most every editorial cartoon that gets published. Usually that person is the only editorial cartoonist in town.

Knowing this is how cartoonists work, some folks objected to the headline in our newspaper on April 16th that read, "P-I wins Pulitzer." They said the win was mine, not the newspaper's. Well, that just isn't so. One man show though it may be, there's just no way this cartoonist could have risen so high without the support of my newspaper and the men and women who put it together every day, in particular J.D. Alexander, the guy who runs the P-I, and Joann Byrd, the P-I's editorial page editor — the gal who runs me. J.D. and Joann were indispensable in putting me over the top. They seldom told me no and they got me where I needed to go. They earned their share of the Pulitzer.

There's plenty of prize to go around — to my editors and colleagues past and present, to my wife, to my children, to my sister, to my friends, to my city and, of course, to that woman who taught me to expect success, my mom.

Oops. Here come those tears again.

*(First printed in Washington Law &
Politics magazine, August 1999.)*

A PORTRAIT OF THE ARTIST

as a Pulitzer Prize Winner

By Erik Lundegaard

For an entire month Sharon Diel of
Seattle had to listen to people laughing
behind her back. She didn't mind,
however. In fact she enjoyed it.

Mrs. Diel, 48, works at the Central
Library in downtown Seattle, and in
June the library honored
*The Seattle Post-
Intelligencer's* David
Horsey, who was
awarded the Pulitzer
Prize for editorial
cartooning on April 12,
1999, by exhibiting 40 or
so of his cartoons on a
large partition in the
center of the main floor
of the library — right
behind Mrs. Diel's information desk.
Many of the cartoons highlighted
President Clinton's very public private
failings over the past year, and their
often ironic repercussions in the
political realm. Example: President
Clinton as Peter Pan slipping through the
jaws of a crocodile (the '98 election),
which instead swallows a fist-shaking
Captain Hook (Newt Gingrich), while a
hefty Tinkerbell (Monica) sparkles
nearby. Clinton: "Golly! Maybe I really
don't have to ever grow up!"

"It made my whole month fun," Mrs.
Diel says of the cartoons and the
laughter that accompanied them. "It
perked up the entire library."

On the last day of the month, Horsey
himself made an appearance at the
library for a noon-hour poster-signing
that quickly turned into a love fest.
Sarah Sharpe, Horsey's colleague at the
Sammamish Valley News in the mid-70s,
was the first of a half-dozen people to
hug him. Tom Adair, 45, took the day off
from work to accompany his step-
daughter, Lindsey Powers of Kent Lake
High School, who is interested in a
possible journalism career. Even readers
who don't necessarily agree with
Horsey's politics were complimentary.
"He's obviously quite liberal," says John
Allerton, 72, of Seattle, "and in spite of
that he criticized Clinton vigorously —
to the point of cruelty — and I didn't
expect him to. It showed independence
and integrity."

About 50 people waited on line, each
with a poster or three to sign, each with
an emphatic compliment. One man
asked Horsey if he was tired of drawing
Monica Lewinsky. "Not yet," Horsey
responded after a pregnant, mischievous
pause. At one point Horsey suggested
that questions might best be answered

during the Q&A following the poster-signing, but the questions still came, and he still answered them, attentive, self-deprecating, as at ease with the crowd as, well, President Clinton would be. He still submitted to the Q&A afterwards.

The library greet-and-meet took a three hour chunk out of his workday. On top of that he had to contend with a roving interview (this one), which itself was interrupted by a tour group of University of Washington students who tossed questions at him for 20 minutes.

"Life's been like this ever since I won the Pulitzer," Horsey told the students with a smile. "I haven't actually done a decent cartoon in months."

Killing Them With Laughter

The seeming contradiction of David Horsey is this: He's an incredibly nice guy, who, in his editorial cartoons, regularly socks it to politicians. Yet they love him for it. He's got a "laser wit," they say. He's a "Washington state icon." The encomiums come so fast and furious that one wonders if Horsey is still alive.

"Dave has this incredible ability to ridicule someone, just *nail* them," says *Seattle Times* editorial writer Casey Corr, one of Horsey's best friends, "and then the person he lampooned wants a copy of the cartoon. I've gone to politicians' offices, and they'll have these incredible Horsey skewerings on their wall. As a writer I'm really jealous of that ability to capture someone and lampoon them in a way that ... they don't want to kill you. They laugh."

And they buy. Politicians on both sides of the political fence are regular customers for Horsey originals, which sell anywhere from $200 to $400. (Pam Roach, R-Auburn, jokingly fears the price will rise now that Horsey's got his Pulitzer.)

U.S. Rep. Jennifer Dunn, a Republican, is Horsey's most frequent customer. "I consider him an interior decorator for my office," Dunn says with a laugh. "Instead of all those ego pictures people usually put up, we've got all these Horsey editorial cartoons." She adds, "They're going to be my dowry someday."

Democratic Governor Gary Locke, who has four Horseys hanging in his office in Olympia, thinks Horsey has a great way of capturing the idiosyncrasies of politicians and government officials-that his cartoons serve almost as a bridge between government perception and popular perception. "As government people," Locke says, "when we see his editorial cartoons, it makes us wonder. *Geez, is that how we're coming off to the public?*"

Even Republican Sen. Slade Gorton is a fan, according to his communications director Rob Nichols. "[David Horsey] can poke fun at you without being mean-spirited," Nichols explains. "And he's got a great grasp of the regional issues that are so peculiar and particular to the Northwest."

Does it bother Horsey that politicians aren't all that bothered by his sharp jabs?

It *surprises* him, certainly. Yet he knows it's all part of the game. "[Politicians] are used to being picked on," he says. "They all have healthy egos and so are flattered by the attention." Occasionally he can still get a rise out of a lawmaker. Recently Horsey visited Olympia where the state Senate read a resolution honoring him for his Pulitzer. Procedure dictated they vote on the resolution first — a voice vote, a formality. "There was one very loud nay," Horsey remembers. "It was a senator I had slammed because he had scuttled a gun control bill. Jim Hargrove." Yet even Hargrove was grinning when he cast his dissenting vote; and of course the resolution passed overwhelmingly.

Horsey, tall and thin, appears young

April 24, 1999 — As the artist responds to accolades from the Washington State Senate, his wife, Nole Ann Ulery-Horsey does a skilled impression of a political spouse.

for his age, which is nearing the half-century mark. His tone is light and jokey, and he'll often comment ironically on what he's just said. This may be a by-product of being interviewed, but it comes across, appropriately enough, like Punk the penguin in Pat Oliphant's editorial cartoons commenting upon the action in the cartoon. Overall Horsey seems so open and unaffected that you feel comfortable in his presence. One thinks of editorial cartoonists as a cloistered, ink-stained sect, but Horsey is a natural in front of a crowd, or on radio, or even on television. Post-Pulitzer, he made a memorable appearance on KING-TV'S *Almost Live,* in which he proudly showed off his prize-winning cartoons — in reality, stick figures penned by writer Pat Cashman — while a perplexed John Keister, the host of the show, looked on. Horsey seemed even more natural on stage than Keister, who does such things for a living.

"I've never had stage fright," Horsey contends. "I just remember thinking, 'Gee, shouldn't I be [nervous]?' I was up, which is a form of nervousness." In a self-mocking tone, he adds, "I had confidence in the material."

A typical workday for Horsey begins with the tail end of the 9 a.m. editorial meeting at the *P-I.* Although his presence isn't required, Horsey's editor, Joann Byrd, likes him on board because of what he can add to the discussion. "He's just smart as the devil," she says.

It's Horsey's hope that the meeting will give him a kernel of an idea. Editorial cartoonists are like columnists in that both are desperate for inspiration, picking at whatever's in the news like birds picking at crumbs along the sidewalk. Sometimes the meeting will give him something to nibble on, but more often than not he returns to his third floor office and reads the *P-I* or the *Times,* or one of the many publications he subscribes to: *The Atlantic Monthly, Vanity Fair, Time, The Wall Street Journal, The New York Times* (Sunday), *Newsweek*.

"What I'm looking for is an issue that's been advanced somehow," Horsey says, "or the top news of the day, or maybe just ... a hot issue that's been on people's minds. I'll often make a list. Just write down three or four topics. Then," he adds anticlimactically, "I sit here a lot."

The image of crumpled paper balls overflowing a wastebasket is not accurate in Horsey's case. Most of the work goes on in his mind. He'll stare out his office window, which overlooks several dilapidated buildings on the northwestern edge of downtown Seattle, or he'll go for a walk or a drive and wait for an image to pop into his head-a visual metaphor for the issue of the day. "[It's] a mysterious, weird process that I can't explain and that I keep worrying will stop. Sometimes something pops up right away. Sometimes I'm still sitting here at 5 o'clock in the afternoon. I can go as late as 7:30 [and still make deadline], but I don't like doing that because I don't want to be here that late."

The day before our interview the big story in the papers was President Clinton's projected trillion dollar federal budget surplus. "I just thought, 'This is

another example of his amazing luck,'" Horsey says. "Everyone said if we went to war in Kosovo it'd be a disaster, it'd be another Vietnam, but somehow he managed to bring it off without losing anybody. Infuriating the Republicans because he was impeached and nobody cares. He's still the President. So this was the latest thing."

Horsey cast the President as a very successful magician. "And the audience, Republicans, is getting sick of it. *One trick after another!*"

After Horsey sketches the idea he shows it to his editor, who may make a suggestion, or excise a nasty Clintonian cigar, but generally waves him along. "Part of my job with Dave is just to help him do what he does best," Byrd says. "I love his artwork but it's the brain cells behind the artwork that really puts him over the top."

The final process, the drawing and inking stage, takes about two hours; incremental changes are sometimes made. Among Clinton's magic tricks — pulling the surplus rabbit out of his hat and escaping from the Kosovo chains — Horsey adds the "sawing Monica in half" trick and alters the Republican elephant's comment so it resonates more. Horsey may be unassuming about his talents but he takes his work

seriously. "I always know there might be a better [idea] out there."

The next day he does it again. Five times a week. Forty-eight weeks a year.

From a Way to Impress Friends to a Career

Jeanne Horsey remembers her son drawing from age 3 on. "We'd put a couple of phone books on a chair and give him lots of paper," she says. "And then he'd sit for hours and hours."

The drawings, which Mrs. Horsey saved, are indicative of a young boy's mind: pirate ships and baseball and king of the hill; and, prefiguring *Doonsebury*, a child watching television while a pipe-smoking father returns from work. A vague story line is attached to these early etchings. "They were like little movies," Horsey remembers. "One was about an investigative reporter who was constantly getting into fights and capturing criminals. He carried one of those old press cameras with the flashbulb and everything. Don't know if I saw it on TV, but it may have indicated an early inclination toward journalism."

Although in second grade Horsey was already drawing elaborate war scenes with a friend, it wasn't until the hormone-crazed sixth grade that his peers saw the true value of his talents. "They wanted me to draw girls for them," Horsey remembers. *"Can you draw girls? If you could just draw a woman."* He pauses, amused. "I have a friend from Connecticut, and when she was in sixth grade she had a friend who paid her to draw women for him." The story elicits this half-ironic, Oliphantish coda. "Sick little people."

Pat Oliphant was an early influence, as was Ron Cobb, who drew for the underground publications of the day. (Eventually Cobb burned out and migrated to Hollywood, where he helped design the characters for *Star Wars, Alien,* and other films.) The Horsey cartoon style, which most applaud and some denigrate, owes much to Cobb. "He did political cartoons that were just amazingly detailed," Horsey remembers. "I got a book of his work, and pretty much just from trying to emulate [it], I went from a high-school style to this. It really made a difference."

Phys-ed teachers helped, believe it or not. Horsey had a skinny boy's animosity towards them, and often drew them, along with gags about lunchroom food and President Nixon, for the Ingraham High School newspaper. In his second quarter at the University of Washington, Horsey took a weight-training course and — returning to bad habits — drew caricatures of the instructors. One muscle-bound teacher saw Horsey's renderings, and like the future politicians of the state, was more flattered than annoyed. He suggested the young cartoonist go work for the campus newspaper.

Horsey was so successful at *The Daily* that by 1972 they were printing "The Best of Horsey" in their pages; they also interviewed him, in the inbred fashion of college newspapers. Photographs show Horsey bedecked in tight turtleneck, love beads, and, one imagines, hopeless idealism. "I consider myself a graphic artist," he told the paper. "That's my major." And in a comment that causes the adult Horsey to roar with laughter, his younger self opined, "I can't see myself spending my life in an office ... I don't want to be working for a bunch of fat old men in an office all day long."

Besides his talent, what set the young Horsey apart on the radicalized campuses of the early 1970s were his religious beliefs. Just a few years earlier a *Time* magazine cover story asked, "Is God dead?" Not to Horsey. One *Daily* cartoon features "Cynicism" questioning a smiling "God." "And what are you smiling about?" Cynicism asks.

"Very straight-laced for the college times of those days," *Seattle Times'* columnist, and one-time *Daily* editor, Erik Lacitis remembers. "I have a faint recollection of one time going to his folks' house. Very Christian. I remembered how nice it was."

"Actually, yeah, in my college years I was pretty active in the evangelical church," Horsey recalls. "There was ... a group calling themselves r*adical Christians* that came to an anti-war stance *through* their religious beliefs. I identified with that a lot."

In 1974 Horsey was elected editor of *The Daily* and pledged more investigative journalism. Later that year he self-published a book of editorial cartoons, *Politics and Other Perversions,* which sold about 1,000 copies. Ray Collins, then-cartoonist for the *P-I,* called Horsey "The best political cartoonist in the history of the University of Washington."

"I was so new to it," Horsey shrugs over his early work. "I didn't know how to do it, I never thought about doing it, and so I was making it up as I went along. Sometimes that's not a bad place to start."

After graduating in 1976, Horsey covered the state legislature as a reporter for the *Daily Journal American* in

Bellevue. Three years later the *P-I* came calling.

You Can Find Him At the P-I

Editorial cartoons are by their very nature reductive: A complex issue is reduced to simple, understandable terms, which, of course, can lead to inexactitude and controversy. One hundred years ago it was common for editorial cartoonists to engage in the worst forms of racial stereotyping, and even mid-century the medium relied on heavy symbolism to get its points across. Pat Oliphant, Horsey feels, helped revolutionize the art form in the 1960s. "I see [editorial cartooning] as more cinematic now," he says. "You create a scene. It's almost as if you're telling a story and this is one moment in the story."

Which doesn't mean that Horsey hasn't gotten himself into trouble — particularly in a PC city like Seattle.

"When I first started at the *P-I* I did a cartoon about the Tacoma Dome," Horsey remembers. "They'd just passed a bond issue to build the Dome. This was right in the middle of various scandals down there involving gambling, corrupt police, so I did a

May 1, 1999 — Nole Ann is wedged between two egos as the artist comes face-to-face with his favorite subject, President Bill Clinton, at the White House Correspondents Dinner.

drawing of what their Dome would be like: smokestack coming out of it, topless dancing ... It got a huge reaction because what I hadn't anticipated was how folks in Tacoma have a real sensitivity to people in Seattle criticizing them. We were inundated."

More likely subjects to draw the ire of angry readers are race and religion. In 1992, a four-paneled Horsey cartoon, in which a white skinhead and a black gangster rapper put aside their differences to find common ground — their mutual hatred of Japanese and

Koreans — was labeled "divisive" by the Washington Commission on African-American Affairs. Recently, the fact that Vatican officials objected more strongly to the use of "morning-after" pills for raped Albanian women than to the atrocities themselves became grist for Horsey's mill — and the P-I was again swamped with letters. Incensed Catholic readers labeled Horsey a "bigot" — ironic given the fact that, after several years of spiritual searching (and to the puzzlement of his friends), he now considers himself a Catholic.

"My response [to the readers] was that attacking the Vatican was not the same as attacking all Catholics everywhere. If any church is involved in the political arena, which they have a right to be, they also leave themselves open to being part of the debate, the criticism."

Some grumble, too, about Horsey's depiction of women. Not his political stance towards women — he's practically a feminist — but his sometime prurient interest in their form. A female colleague in D.C. complained about the number of buxom women in his work, which sent Horsey searching through his drawings over the last two years. He discovered, in his favor, that the only semi-buxom woman he'd drawn was Monica Lewinsky, "who is, of course, fairly buxom." Nevertheless, Horsey's not above giving even Linda Tripp a leggy thigh, which is a great stretch of any male imagination.

None of this has stopped *The Seattle Times* from trying to pry him away from their rival newspaper — particularly because the *Times*, in changing from an afternoon to a morning newspaper, is moving into direct competition with the *P-I*. The *Times* tried to reel Horsey in but he didn't bite. "He was brilliant until the day he turned down the opportunity to work for *The Seattle Times*," jokes his friend, Corr. "From then on he's dirt."

Horsey jabs back. If the *P-I* went under would he consider working for the *Times*, which has not had the best record with editorial cartoonists? (Their last two were dismissed under acrimonious circumstances, and they've been without a regular cartoonist for years.) "Well, I'd certainly need a job," Horsey begins. "But ... I would hope I could do better."

Of the rivalry between the papers — friendship notwithstanding — Horsey says simply, "They would like to bury us, we'd like to bury them."

"Obviously a rivalry exists between the *Times* and *P-I*," explains Ross Anderson, environmental reporter for the *Times*. "But there's people like Horsey, Joni Balter, my wife Mary Rothschild, all of them went to school at the UW together and worked on *The Daily* together ... The camaraderie among us is more powerful than any legitimate — and it is legitimate — rivalry between the papers."

The Clinton of Cartoonists

Horsey's first post-Pulitzer cartoon shows his dumbfounded self sitting slumped at the easel worrying over what he might possibly do next. It's a good question. He's published four books of political cartoons, he's syndicated in more 450 newspapers, he's got awards up the ying-yang. He's married with two children: Darielle, 16, and Daniel, 15. In 1986, he and his family spent a year in England, where he earned a master's in international relations from the University of Kent at Canterbury. That same year he began a daily comic strip, *Boomer's Song*, which didn't last the decade but which he feels taught him a lot. In 1995, he uprooted his family again and spent a year in D.C. He may be the most well-traveled cartoonist in the country, having been to Europe and Asia, and having covered, as a cartoonist, political campaigns, conventions, Olympics and the opening of Safeco Field. This autumn he will head down to LA to figure out what makes Hollywood, that purveyor of worldwide culture, tick.

"He's the most artful manipulator of editors I've ever known," Corr says. "He can go up to an editor and say, 'I want to go to New York and stay at the Plaza to do a series of insights on how the hotel industry has affected politics, and I'll have to have chocolate mousse every day,' and they'll say, '*Dave!* I've been *waiting* for someone to suggest that idea!'"

Horsey owns up to this talent; he even admits to similarities with his most famous subject.

"Not in as dramatic or blatant a way as Bill Clinton," Horsey says, "but I think I've gotten away with a lot in my life by being charming, or having talent or people skills. Half the time I feel like I'm getting away with something just doing this job. It's mostly fun. I get paid well and get all kinds of credit for doing this thing that's just fun to do, and that I did when I was 5 years old.

"I've been lucky like Bill Clinton has been lucky," he continues. "He has a scale of luck that's pretty unbelievable but maybe *mine* is in a different way. Things have always worked out well for me."

—*Erik Lundegaard is a regular contributor to* Law & Politics *and also writes for* The New York Times Magazine, *the* Utne Reader, The Seattle Times *and* The Grand Salami, *a* Seattle Mariners *magazine.*

A BRIEF HISTORY of the MILLENNIUM

One misty morning a thousand years ago, Leif Erickson discovered America. Of course, he didn't know what he had done so, hungry for a bit of home-cooked lutefisk, he sailed back home. . .

The truth is, not much else happened for the first half of the millennium. Most people on the planet were peasants with no money and a short life expectancy. Plus, they were bored to tears...

The world's peasant majority lived at the whim of psychopathic killers and thieves. These unpleasant gangsters went by different names in different cultures: kings, princes, dukes, emperors, conquerors, caliphs, sultans, chiefs. Among them, there was Tamerlane in central Asia who loved to pile up the severed heads of his victims. There were the Aztec rulers who, on one particular day, cut out the hearts of 20,000 captives. And there was Mensa Musa, the African king, who executed anyone who dared to sneeze in his presence...

Genghis Khan was the greatest gang leader. His turf stretched from China to the edges of Europe and still he was unsatisfied...

These ruling gangs spent most of their time fighting each other. The Christian gang spent years and years battling the Muslim gang for turf in the Holy Land...

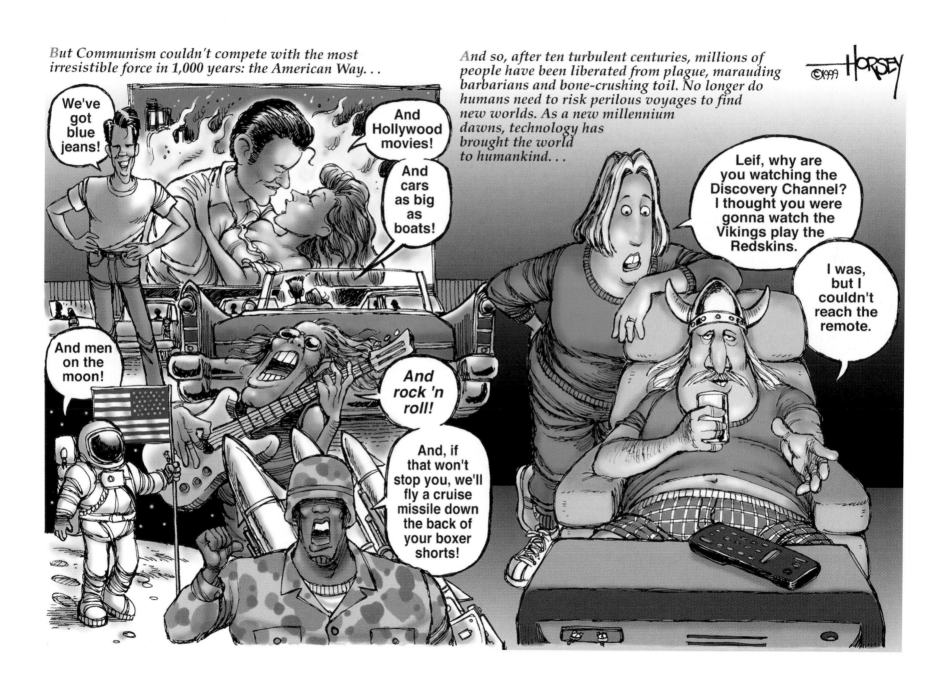

BELTWAY APOCALYPSE

How a bill becomes law in the 104th Congress

THE DEBATE, THUS FAR...

My Visit to Washington, D.C.

me

My Dad took me to visit Washington, D.C., because he said there was lots of FREE stuff to do like talking to the people who represent me in the government...

senator

Golfing for $

First we went to see our senator but he was in FLORIDA golfing with some guys who gave TONS of money to his re-election campaign...

Then we went to meet our Representative. She shook my hand but had to hurry off to a fundraising dinner...

Time is money, boy!

So we went over to the White House to see the President. A guard told us only people like kings and prime ministers get in, but I knew that wasn't so because I heard about these rich people who paid big money and got to sleep in Lincoln's bed...

1600

What I learned: Maybe there is free stuff in Washington, D.C., but if you want to hang out with the guys you voted into office, better bring GOBS of money!! ☆$$$$☆

©1997 SEATTLE POST-INTELLIGENCER
NORTH AMERICA SYNDICATE

HORSEY

· JUDGMENT CALL ·

BOB DOLE, THE MORNING AFTER THE LATEST POLL...

MONDALE '84

©1996
SEATTLE POST-
INTELLIGENCER
NORTH AMERICA
SYNDICATE

HORSEY

"MY *HUSBAND*, NOW *HE'S FULL* OF OPINIONS...TOO BAD HE'S AT DRUG REHAB' THIS MONTH. MY *FIRST* HUSBAND'S A KNOW-IT-ALL, TOO, BUT HE'S LIVING WITH HIS BOYFRIEND IN SAN FRANCISCO. COME BACK TOMORROW AND YOU CAN INTERVIEW MY 18-YEAR-OLD. I'M BABYSITTING HER KIDS HERE WHILE SHE DOES HER SHIFT AT THE *TOPLESS JOINT.* ...BUT, ANYWAY, IF YOU *REALLY* WANT *MY* OPINION: *NO, THE CHARACTER ISSUE IS NO BIG DEAL!*"

"I'M FRED THOMPSON FROM THE *VICE SQUAD!* PLEASE, GO ON ABOUT YOUR BUSINESS, SENATOR, I'VE JUST GOT TO CHECK UNDER THE BED FOR ANY *UNSAVORY CHINESE!*"

"THIS SECOND DATE WOULD'VE BEEN A *LOT* MORE FUN IF YOU HADN'T BROUGHT A *CHAPERONE!*"

"FINALLY! A REAL BITE!"

"HON', I CAN'T DECIDE WHAT TO WEAR TONIGHT... THE TIE FROM KATHLEEN WILLEY OR THE TIE FROM MONICA."

BIGGER THAN TITANIC...

"...PAULA, KEN, KATHLEEN, MONICA, MR. GINSBURG, MS. TRIPP -- GOSH! THERE ARE JUST SO MANY FOLKS WHO HELPED MAKE MY *PRIVATE LIFE* THE *NUMBER ONE ENTERTAINMENT* OF THE YEAR!"

"SURE, I'LL TESTIFY TO KEN STARR, BUT *ONLY* IN A MANNER THAT PRESERVES THE *DIGNITY* OF THE *PRESIDENCY!*"

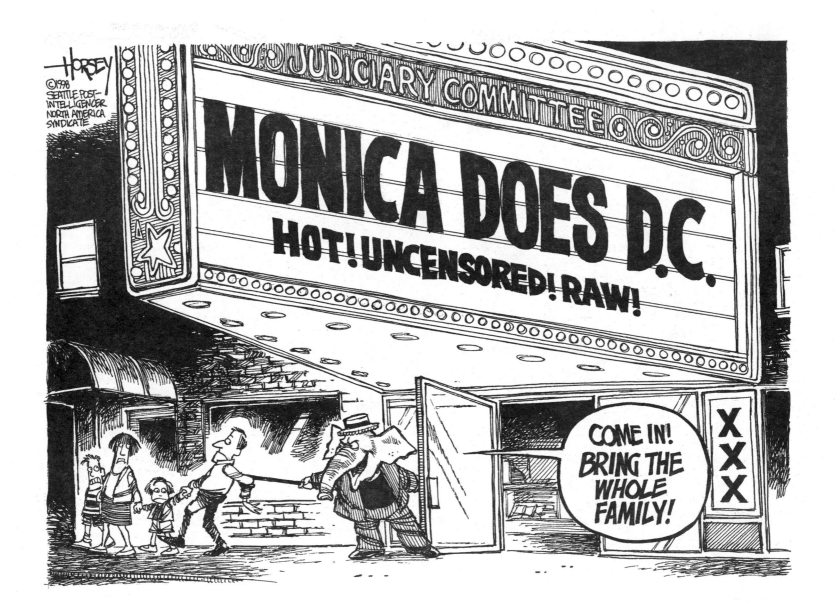

"EMPTIES! NOTHING BUT EMPTIES! HOW'M I (HIC) SHUPPOSED TO (URP) KEEP A GOOD BUZZ ON?!"

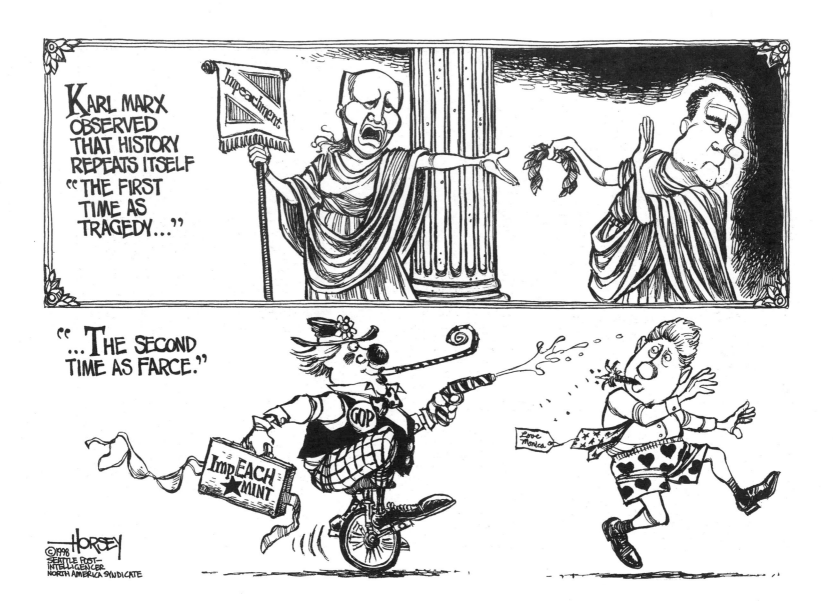

As the

CENTURY
TURNS

AMERICA, 1999: WHAT'S WRONG WITH THIS PICTURE?

"HOP IN, KID! WE'LL GO TO A MOVIE, WATCH A LITTLE TV, LISTEN TO SOME MUSIC...
YOUR MOM AND DAD WON'T EVEN HAVE TO KNOW!"

THE MEDIA FOOD CHAIN:

The rat eats the slug...

DICK MORRIS AND OTHER PROSTITUTES

TABLOIDS

...the skunk eats the rat...

TV

...the badger eats the skunk...

NEWSPAPERS

...and so on.

BOOK PUBLISHERS

COULD YOU SUGGEST A WINE TO GO WITH MY MEAL?

Horsey
©1996
SEATTLE POST-
INTELLIGENCER
NORTH AMERICA SYNDICATE

"LEIF! STOP AND THINK HOW THAT MIGHT AFFECT YOUR *MILITARY CAREER!*"

"OOPS, MY MISTAKE... IT'S *VIAGRA*, HAROLD, *VIAGRA*!"

Woodstock Generation...

©1994 SEATTLE POST-INTELLIGENCER
NORTH AMERICA SYNDICATE

HORSEY

1969
TURNED ON
TUNED IN
DROPPED OUT

1981
SOLD OUT
BOUGHT IN
SNUFFED UP

1994
DRIED OUT
TUNED IN
TICKED OFF

"I CHANGED THE NAME FIGURIN' TO CASH IN ON THE CURRENT MOOD OF THE MARKET...WENT *PUBLIC*...GOT *LISTED* ON THE *NASDAQ*... AND THE STOCK PRICE *QUADRUPLED* SINCE *TUESDAY!*"

"MAYBE WE'D BE *SAFER* JUST HANGING OUT ON THE *STREET* UNTIL MOM COMES HOME..."

"THEY TELL ME I SHOULD FEEL GOOD ABOUT THE COMPETITION!"

· A WIN-WIN SITUATION ·

THE FLAW IN THE BOMBING PLAN...

BEFORE

AFTER

"AS YOU REQUESTED, A ROOM WITH T.V.!"

A MIRACLE, AMERICAN STYLE

"JENNIFER STAYED AT THE *HOUSE*... *I'M* YOUR DATE!"

"I STAND IN SOLIDARITY WITH NATIVE PEOPLES DEFENDING THEIR HERITAGE FROM WHITE MALE CULTURAL *HEGEMONY!*"

"I ALSO CONDEMN *SPECIES CHAUVINISTS* WHO THINK IT'S O.K. TO MURDER SENTIENT, NON-HUMAN CREATURES!"

"IN *OTHER* WORDS, I SUPPORT THE NATIVE AMERICAN *WHALE HUNTERS...*"

© 1998 SEATTLE POST-INTELLIGENCER
NORTH AMERICA SYNDICATE

HORSEY

"...BUT I WANT TO *SAVE THE WHALES!*"

"NATIVES? WHALES? WHALES? NATIVES?"

"*OUCH!* I THINK I'VE GOT A *POLITICAL CORRECTNESS MIGRAINE!*"

A SEATTLE HALLOWEEN

ALL DRESSED UP WITH NO PLACE TO GO...

MAYOR SCHELL WANTS TO ILLUMINATE SEATTLE'S BRIDGES TO USHER IN THE MILLENIUM...

HERE'S A BETTER IDEA...

HAPPY NEW YEAR, HONEY... GOSH! AREN'T THE POTHOLES JUST GORGEOUS TONIGHT?

THE ARRIVAL OF CHARLIE CHONG...

Seattle City Council

Politics can be such fun. But this year, the race for mayor of Seattle has been reduced to an endless series of obscure community forums where candidates say the same thing, over and over and over and over. . .

Is it any wonder voters pay more attention to differences between microbrews than differences between the candidates? Charlie Chong and Paul Schell are actually quite intriguing chaps. If only we could see them as they really are. If only we could have. . .

THE VIRTUAL CAMPAIGN

In the virtual campaign, candidates say just what's on their minds, unrestrained by handlers and timid tacticians...

ACTUALLY, I'D LIKE TO SEE ANYONE WHO HAS MOVED HERE SINCE 1987 DRIVEN INTO THE COUNTRYSIDE AT THE POINT OF A BAYONET!

ACTUALLY, I'D LIKE TO FLY TO FRANCE AND NOT COME BACK TILL THE ELECTION'S OVER.

The virtual campaign ad for Charlie Chong...

ARE YOU READY TO ABANDON THE KIDS, TRADE THE MINIVAN FOR A HARLEY AND HEAD TO VEGAS TO BLOW A PILE OF PAYCHECKS ON ONE ROLL OF THE DICE?! THEN YOU'RE READY FOR CHARLIE!...

TAKE A LEAP! VOTE CHONG!

In the virtual campaign, the candidates forge into alien territory to court new constituencies...

I WANT TO ENSURE A BRIGHT FUTURE FOR YOUNG PEOPLE LIKE YOU!

FUTURE? I'M MORE, LIKE, INTO DEATH.

DEATH. YEAH, COOL.

CAN I BRING YOU ANYTHING, MR. CHONG?

RAINIER CLUB

MOLOTOV COCKTAIL, PLEASE.

ONE ~finis~ SHOW